MATHWORKS!

Using Math to Conquer EXTREME SPORTS

GARETH STEVENS
GS
PUBLISHING
A World Almanac Education Group Company

by
**Wendy and David Clemson,
Oli Cundale, Laura Berry, and Matt King**

Please visit our web site at: www.garethstevens.com
For a free color catalog describing Gareth Stevens Publishing's
list of high-quality books and multimedia programs, call
1-800-542-2595 (USA) or 1-800-387-3178 (Canada).
Gareth Stevens Publishing's fax: (414) 332-3567.

Library of Congress Cataloging-in-Publication Data

Clemson, Wendy.
   Using math to conquer extreme sports / by Wendy
Clemson . . . [et al.]. — North American ed.
      p. cm. — (Mathworks!)
   ISBN 0-8368-4210-3 (lib. bdg.)
      1. Mathematics—Problems, exercises, etc.—Juvenile
literature.   2. Extreme sports—Juvenile literature.
   I. Clemson, Wendy.   II. Series.
   QA43.U85   2004
   510'.76—dc22   2004045438

This North American edition first published in 2005 by
Gareth Stevens Publishing
A World Almanac Education Group Company
330 West Olive Street, Suite 100
Milwaukee, Wisconsin 53212

This U.S. edition copyright © 2005 by Gareth Stevens, Inc.
Original edition copyright © 2004 by ticktock Entertainment
Ltd. First published in Great Britain in 2004 by ticktock Media
Ltd., Unit 2, Orchard Business Centre, North Farm Road,
Tunbridge Wells, Kent, TN2 3XF, United Kingdom.

The publishers thank the following consultants for their kind
assistance: Jenni Back and Liz Pumfrey (NRICH Project,
Cambridge University) and Debra Voege.

Gareth Stevens Editor: Jim Mezzanotte
Gareth Stevens Art Direction: Tammy West

Photo credits (t=top, b=bottom, c=center, l=left, r=right)
Alamy: cover, 2-3, 6(cr), 7(bl), 8-9, 10-11, 12, 14-15,
17(t, br), 18-19, 20-21, 24-25(t), 26(cr), 26-27(c), 27(tl, tr, cr).
TheBoarder.co.uk: 6-7, 15(b), 27(bl). Anna Bond (Matt King): 1.
Corbis: 19(tr). The Friedman Archives (Gary Friedman): 17(c),
22-23. www.dopeshots.com: 24-25(b).

Every effort has been made to trace the copyright holders
for the photos used in this book. The publisher apologizes,
in advance, for any unintentional omissions and would be
pleased to insert the appropriate acknowledgements in
any subsequent edition of this publication.

Printed in the United States of America

1 2 3 4 5 6 7 8 9 08 07 06 05 04

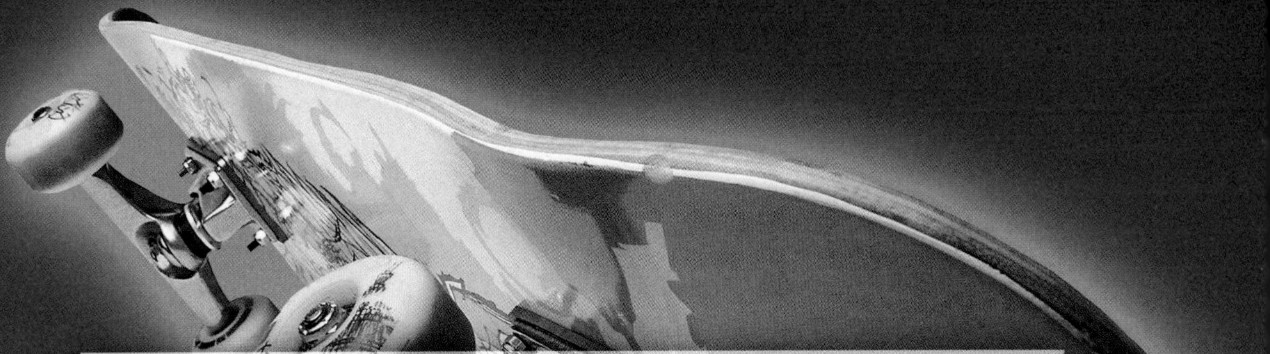

CONTENTS

HAVE FUN WITH MATH (How to Use This Book)   4

GOING TO EXTREMES   6

SKATEBOARDING WITH OLI   8

INLINE SKATING WITH MATT   10

SNOWBOARDING WITH LAURA   12

PRACTICE MAKES PERFECT   14

STREET COMPETITIONS   16

THE NEED FOR SPEED   18

EXTREME SLOPES   20

REACH FOR THE SKY   22

THE EXTREME SPORTS CENTER   24

THE EXTREME SPORTS CHALLENGE   26

MATH TIPS   28

ANSWERS   30

GLOSSARY/MEASUREMENT CONVERSIONS   32

WARNING

This book is not intended to be a training manual for skateboarding, snowboarding, or inline skating.
Before attempting tricks on a skateboard, snowboard, or pair of inline skates, take lessons from a
professional instructor and ALWAYS wear the correct protective clothing.

The extreme tricks and stunts featured in this book have been performed by professional, highly experienced
sports men and women. Read about them and say "WOW," but, under no circumstances, try the tricks yourselves!
If you do, don't blame us — **WE TOLD YOU NOT TO TRY IT!**

(Neither the publishers nor the authors will be liable for any bodily harm or damage to property
that may be sustained or caused as a result of conducting any of the activities featured in this book.)

HAVE FUN WITH MATH

How to Use This Book

Math is important in the daily lives of people everywhere. We use math when we play games, ride bicycles, or go shopping, and everyone uses math when they take part in sports. Imagine you are a top extreme sports athlete. You may not realize it, but when you set a new world record you are using math! In this book, you will be able to try lots of exciting math activities as you check out some thrilling and dangerous tricks and stunts. If you can work with numbers, shapes, measurements, charts, and diagrams, then you could **CONQUER EXTREME SPORTS.**

How does it feel to land a trick?

Grab your skates or boards and find out what it is like to break world records.

Math Activities

The sports clipboards have math activities for you to try. Get your pencil, ruler, and notebook (for figuring out problems and listing answers).

SNOWBOARDING WITH LAURA

Laura says, "Snowboarding is exciting and fun, and it gives me a buzz! I get to travel all over the world, meet new people, and make new friends. As long as everybody is having fun, riders of all abilities will snowboard together, offering each other encouragement and helping each other progress and improve. I personally love to ride anywhere that has big air jumps, super-pipes, and technical rails. Snowboarding competitions can take place on mountains, at indoor snow slopes, and on dry slopes. There are lots of different types of snowboarding competitions — pipe, big air, snowboarder-cross, and slopestyle."

halfpipe

Go For It!

It is the final of a halfpipe competition. A halfpipe is made of snow and looks like a giant pipe that has been cut in half. The snowboarders ride down the pipe performing tricks. They are awarded points in four categories, with 10 being the highest possible score in each category. The rider with the highest total score is the winner.

the lip

The DATA BOX on page 13 has the scores of six halfpipe finalists.

1) Who got the lowest total score?
2) Who did better than Rob in both amplitude and overall impression?
3) Who got the same score as Zak?
4) How many people had final scores that were odd numbers?
5) Who got the highest score and won the halfpipe competition?

Competition Facts

In snowboarder-cross, riders race downhill around and over obstacles. Courses can be a half mile in length. The riders race in groups of six, with the fastest rider in each group going on to a final. In the final, the first rider to reach the bottom wins gold!

12

4

NEED HELP?

- **If you are not sure how to do some of the math problems, turn to pages 28 and 29, where you will find lots of tips to help get you started.**

- **Turn to pages 30 and 31 to check your answers. (Try all the activities and challenges before you look at the answers.)**

- **Turn to page 32 for definitions of some words and terms used in this book.**

Have fun, but stay safe!

Skateboarders, inline skaters, and snowboarders must always follow these important safety rules:

- Wear a helmet at all times and make sure it fits snugly.
- Wear knee pads, elbow pads, and gloves. Inline skaters should wear wrist guards, too.
- Wear reflective clothing if you are skateboarding or skating after sunset.
- Take some lessons. A qualified instructor will teach you the basics and make sure you know what you are doing.
- Never try a trick that is beyond your level. There is a fine line between being confident and being foolish! Start small and build up slowly.
- Always do these sports with friends. It's more fun, and if one of you gets injured, someone is there to go for help.

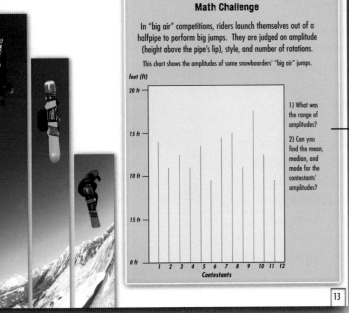

DATA BOX	HALFPIPE SCORES (POINTS OUT OF 40)			
NAME	STANDARD AIRS	ROTATIONS	AMPLITUDE	OVERALL IMPRESSION
Lyn	5	9	8	4
Rob	8	8	7	8
Ahmed	6	9	6	9
Laura	9	8	8	7
Zak	7	7	8	9
Alli	8	5	5	5

- *STANDARD AIRS:* Tricks and movements such as grabs.
- *ROTATIONS* (spins and flips): 180°, 360° (a full spin), 540°, 720°, 900°, 1080°, 1260°.
- *AMPLITUDE:* The height the rider reaches above the lip of the pipe.
- *OVERALL IMPRESSION:* Style, level of difficulty of tricks, creativity and landings.

Trick Facts

The highest "air" ever achieved is 30 feet above the lip of the pipe. The longest-spinning jump ever done is a 1260 (1,260°, or three and a half full spins while in the air).

Math Challenge

In "big air" competitions, riders launch themselves out of a halfpipe to perform big jumps. They are judged on amplitude (height above the pipe's lip), style, and number of rotations.

This chart shows the amplitudes of some snowboarders' "big air" jumps.

feet (ft)

1) What was the range of amplitudes?

2) Can you find the mean, median, and mode for the contestants' amplitudes?

Contestants

Math Facts and Data

To complete some of the math activities, you will need information from a DATA BOX, which looks like this.

Math Challenges

Green boxes, like this one, have extra math questions to challenge you. Give them a try!

You will find lots of amazing details about skateboarding, inline skating, and snowboarding in FACT boxes that look like this.

Skateboarding, inline skating, and snowboarding are extreme sports. The highly skilled athletes who take part are able to perform amazing and dangerous moves that seem impossible to do! In this book, you will read about the top tricks and the most breathtaking stunts in extreme sports. You will find out who can jump the highest, who can fly through the air the farthest, and who can reach mind-blowing speeds. Check out these sports with our boarders and skaters, Oli, Laura, and Matt, and decide which sport YOU think offers the most extreme thrills.

backside boardslide down a handrail

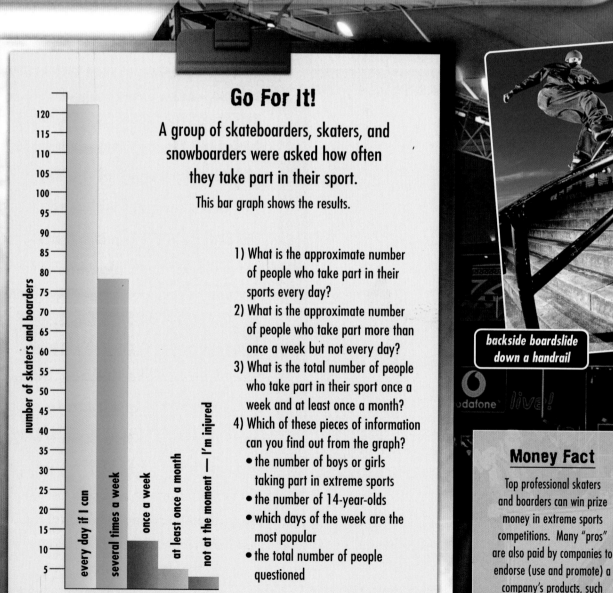

Go For It!

A group of skateboarders, skaters, and snowboarders were asked how often they take part in their sport.

This bar graph shows the results.

1) What is the approximate number of people who take part in their sports every day?
2) What is the approximate number of people who take part more than once a week but not every day?
3) What is the total number of people who take part in their sport once a week and at least once a month?
4) Which of these pieces of information can you find out from the graph?
   • the number of boys or girls taking part in extreme sports
   • the number of 14-year-olds
   • which days of the week are the most popular
   • the total number of people questioned

number of skaters and boarders (y-axis: 5 to 120)

Categories:
- every day if I can
- several times a week
- once a week
- at least once a month
- not at the moment — I'm injured

Money Fact

Top professional skaters and boarders can win prize money in extreme sports competitions. Many "pros" are also paid by companies to endorse (use and promote) a company's products, such as skates, boards, clothes, shoes, hats, helmets, sunglasses, and goggles.

Street Fact

Street skating involves exactly what its name describes. Skateboarders and skaters use everyday obstacles on the street to perform amazing tricks! They ride off curbs and over park benches, and they even ride down stairs and handrails.

Vert Fact

Vert skaters and skateboarders want to go vertical — often up in the air! This type of skating is similar to street skating. The idea is to flip, spin, grab, and slide on your board or skates, but in a bowl, ramp, or halfpipe. Vert skaters go to skate parks or build vert ramps.

Math Challenge

You are preparing for a snowboarding trip and need to choose a new board.

Snowboards come in different sizes to suit the rider's weight, ability, and style of riding.

Here are some snowboard designs to compare. You will see the range of lengths for each design and the prices of the boards.

Board A) Length range: 55 to 61 inches
Price: $530

Board B) Length range: 58 to 63 inches
Price: $618

Board C) Length range: 56 to 60 inches
Price: $576

Board D) Length range: 57 to 62 inches
Price: $608

1) Which board offers the biggest range in length?

2) Which board costs $580 when rounded up to the nearest ten dollars?

Laura Berry rides a rainbow rail.

"Japan air" on a halfpipe

Oli says, "Skateboarding is more than just a sport. There's a whole culture based around it, with companies that produce clothes, shoes, and videos for skateboarders. It's a sport that can give you an enormous sense of satisfaction, and it's also a great way to meet new people. To be a good skateboarder, you need to be athletic and creative. Skateboarding is a very technical sport and takes a lot of skill, and there are hundreds of tricks to learn. The best skateboarders have not only nerve, but dedication, too. Many top tricks can take years of practice to get right!"

Go For It!

Here are some skateboard tricks.

For each of these three tricks, figure out what fraction of a whole turn a skateboarder has to make and how many degrees in the angle of the turn.

POWERSLIDES (tricks 1 and 2):
Shift your weight to one side of the board and slide the back wheels around. A powerslide is a good way to slow down.

SHOVE-IT (trick 3):
Do an Ollie. While you are in the air, spin the board around underneath you.

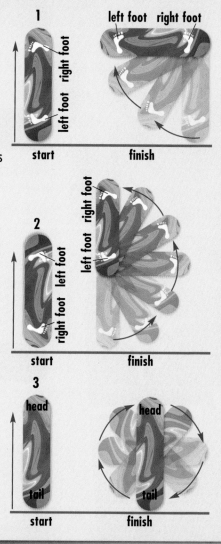

Trick Facts

The basis for most skateboarding tricks is the "Ollie" (invented in the late 1970s by Alan "Ollie" Gelfand). A skater stomps on the tail of the board with the back foot. As the tail hits the ground, the skater hops up off that foot into the air, and the board comes, too! The skater then pushes forward with the front foot, levels the board, and drops to the ground. Skaters can pull Ollies over 3 feet high. It can look as though the board is actually stuck to their feet!

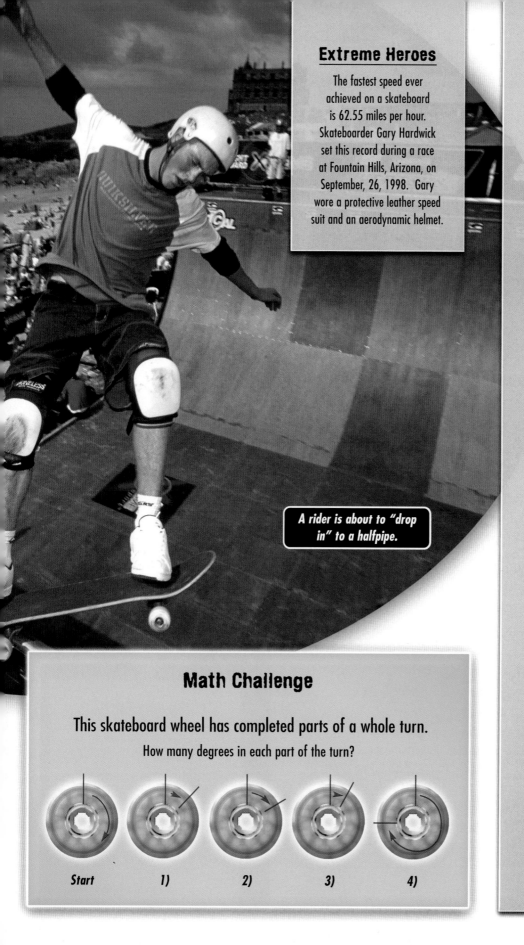

Extreme Heroes

The fastest speed ever achieved on a skateboard is 62.55 miles per hour. Skateboarder Gary Hardwick set this record during a race at Fountain Hills, Arizona, on September, 26, 1998. Gary wore a protective leather speed suit and an aerodynamic helmet.

A rider is about to "drop in" to a halfpipe.

Trick Talk

AIR to jump into the air with a skateboard

FAT (PHAT) a description of a skateboarding trick that is performed over a long distance or to a great height

FLIP a trick in which a board completely flips over and lands back on its wheels

GOOFY skating with your right foot forward

KICKTURN performed on a halfpipe, a trick in which the skateboarder rotates on the rear wheels of the board with the front wheels raised up from the ground

MANUAL traveling on a board by balancing on just the rear wheels (doing a wheelie)

REGULAR skating with your left foot forward

REVERT to finish a trick in a forward direction, then quickly slide around 180˚ to come out backwards

SKETCHY a description of a trick in which the skateboarder is wobbly and just about lands the trick

SWITCHSTANCE skating in the opposite stance (regular or goofy) than the one you normally use

Math Challenge

This skateboard wheel has completed parts of a whole turn.

How many degrees in each part of the turn?

Start   1)   2)   3)   4)

Matt says, "Inline skating offers the adrenaline rush of high speeds and the thrill of performing tricks and stunts. Speed skaters hurtle around race tracks, while 'aggressive skaters' perform jumps, spins, and grabs on street courses or vert ramps. Aggressive skating, or 'rolling,' was started in the early 1990s by a group of extreme sports enthusiasts who felt they just weren't getting the kind of 'rush' they were looking for. Aggressive skating offers incredible thrills. It's also really convenient for beginners, because your skates are attached to your feet so they can't go flying off during a trick like a board can!"

Go For It!

Successful speed skating combines a high level of fitness with good technique and tactics. In sprint races, groups of up to ten skaters race to qualify for the final. Skating at high speeds so closely to other competitors takes a lot of skill.

In the final of a 300-meter sprint race, there were ten skaters. Using their times from the DATA BOX on page 11, answer these questions:

1) How many skaters had a time under 26 seconds?
2) Which skaters had a time over 27 seconds?
3) Would a skater who finished the sprint in 25.3 seconds be ranked 3rd, 11th, or 5th?
4) Three race tracks are holding qualifying races for the first round in a speed-skating competition. If there is a maximum of 10 skaters in a race, how many first-round qualifying races will there be at each location
   - TRACK A: 209 skaters have entered
   - TRACK B: 92 skaters have entered
   - TRACK C: 165 skaters have entered

High speed!

Speed Fact

Matt King has actually been caught speeding on his skates in London! In a daring stunt that was performed on empty roads in the middle of the night, Matt and some friends actually managed to set off a speed camera. To build up their speed at the start of their run, the skaters held on to the back of a sports car. The speed camera photographed them traveling at 80 miles per hour!

DATA BOX

Speed Skater Times

NAME	TIME IN SECONDS
Jolly	25.0
Paul	24.4
Mo	25.2
Josh	27.9
Dec	25.6
Phil	26.3
Ant	30.2
Ian	24.7
Flo	26.8
Dave	31.5

A skater pulls a big "mute air" on a ramp.

TRICK TALK

AIRS These tricks can be performed on street courses or ramps. While "airing," skaters perform spins, flips, and grabs (grabbing their skates).

FLY FISH The right hand grabs the right boot and the right leg is extended, while the left foot stays tucked under the body.

MUTE AIR With the legs tucked up in front of the body, a skater reaches the right hand over both shins to grab the left boot.

ROCKET AIR Both legs are extended out in front of the body. The left hand touches the right toe, or the right hand touches the left toe.

SAFETY GRAB Knees are tucked up so the body is in a ball. The right hand is on the right boot, or the left hand is on the left boot.

LUI KANG Knees are to chest, and left hand is to left foot or right hand is to right foot. Then, the free leg kicks out.

SKATE TALK

FACE PLANT or BAILS hitting your nose to the pavement before your hands!

RASPBERRY the "road rash" you get when your skin scrapes the pavement

PAVEMENT INSPECTORS skaters who are beginners

Math Challenge

An aggressive skater pulls an air on a halfpipe and reaches a height of 13 feet.

1) What is the approximate height in meters?

2) What is the approximate height in meters for:
   a) 11 feet   b) 8 feet   c) 4 feet

BOARDERS

Laura says, "Snowboarding is exciting and fun, and it gives me a buzz! I get to travel all over the world, meet new people, and make new friends. As long as everybody is having fun, riders of all abilities will snowboard together, offering each other encouragement and helping each other progress and improve. I personally love to ride anywhere that has big air jumps, super-pipes, and technical rails. Snowboarding competitions can take place on mountains, at indoor snow slopes, and on dry slopes. There are lots of different types of snowboarding competitions — pipe, big air, snowboarder-cross, and slopestyle."

halfpipe

the lip

Go For It!

It is the final of a halfpipe competition. A halfpipe is made of snow and looks like a giant pipe that has been cut in half. The snowboarders ride down the pipe performing tricks. They are awarded points in four categories, with 10 being the highest possible score in each category. The rider with the highest total score is the winner.

The DATA BOX on page 13 has the scores of six halfpipe finalists.

1) Who got the lowest total score?
2) Who did better than Rob in both amplitude and overall impression?
3) Who got the same score as Zak?
4) How many people had final scores that were odd numbers?
5) Who got the highest score and won the halfpipe competition?

Competition Facts

In snowboarder-cross, riders race downhill around and over obstacles. Courses can be a half mile in length. The riders race in groups of six, with the fastest rider in each group going on to a final. In the final, the first rider to reach the bottom wins gold!

Halfpipe Scores (POINTS OUT OF 40)

NAME	STANDARD AIRS	ROTATIONS	AMPLITUDE	OVERALL IMPRESSION
Lyn	5	9	8	4
Rob	8	8	7	8
Ahmed	6	9	6	9
Laura	9	8	8	7
Zak	7	7	8	9
Alli	8	5	5	5

- **STANDARD AIRS:** tricks and maneuvers, such as grabs
- **ROTATIONS** (spins and flips): 180°, 360° (a full spin), 540°, 720°, 900°, 1,080°, 1,260°
- **AMPLITUDE:** the height that the rider reaches above the lip of the pipe
- **OVERALL IMPRESSION:** style, level of difficulty of tricks, creativity, and landings

Trick Facts

The highest "air" ever achieved is 30 feet above the lip of the pipe. The longest-spinning jump ever done is a 1260 (1,260°, or three and a half full spins while in the air).

Math Challenge

In "big air" competitions, riders launch themselves out of a halfpipe to perform big jumps. They are judged on amplitude (height above the pipe's lip), style, and number of rotations.

This chart shows the amplitudes of some snowboarders' "big air" jumps.

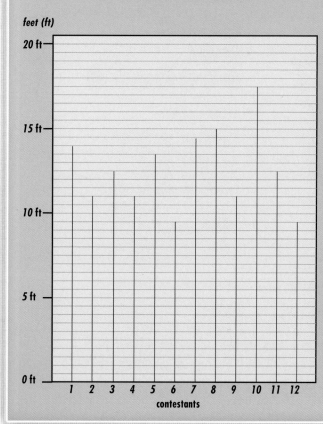

1) What was the range of amplitudes?

2) Can you find the mean, median, and mode for the contestants' amplitudes?

Many top extreme athletes actually turned professional while they were still at school and are now able to make a living from their sport. To keep their places at the top, however, some professionals practice for up to eight hours every day! Oli, Laura, and Matt all agree that the only way to really master all the most impressive tricks and jumps is to practice and practice and then practice again. If you want to be the best, you have to be willing to put in the hours. Of course, if you love your sport, the more time you can spend on your board or skates, the better!

Go For It!

Here are some pictograms showing the number of times some tricks were attempted by a skateboarder, an inline skater, and a snowboarder during one week.

SKATEBOARDER

a) Kickflip

b) 50-50 grind

c) Ollie

= 10 times

= 10 times

= 10 times

INLINE SKATER

a) Mute air

b) Lui Kang

c) Safety grab

SNOWBOARDER

a) Rodeo

b) Frontside 540 melon

c) Backside 180 indy

1) How many times was trick "a" practiced in each sport?
2) How many more times was trick "a" practiced than trick "b" in each sport?
3) How many times did each person practice all the tricks?

(See TRICK TALK in the glossary for more information on these tricks.)

Extreme Heroes

Matt says, "Shane 'Tasmanian Devil' Yost is a professional inline skater famous for his flips and spins. Shane was the first skater to pull a 1260 (a 1,260° spin, or three and a half full turns in midair)."

Extreme Heroes

Laura says, "Snowboarder Jussi Oksanen from Finland is fast becoming a hero to snowboarders everywhere. Jussi has a great style and can spin a 1080 (three full turns, which is 1,080°) in both switchstance and his normal stance."

Extreme Heroes

Oli says, "Tony Hawk is one of the world's most famous skateboarders. He has won hundreds of competitions, invented dozens of tricks, and turned professional when he was fourteen years old. Tony went into skateboarding history when he landed the first ever 900 (two and a half midair turns, which is 900°) at the 1999 X Games."

Tony Hawk pulls a "gymnast plant."

Laura Berry performs a "frontside 540 melon."

Math Challenge

How long does equipment last? Oli says, "A skateboard belonging to a beginner could last a year. But a board belonging to a 'pro,' who practices jumping down a set of twenty steps, might only last for an hour!"

These boards and skates have all been used for hours of tough practicing. They are now worn out or damaged and are no longer in use.

Inline skate wheels lasted:
May and June

Snowboards lasted:
336 hours

Skateboard lasted:
10,080 minutes

1) How long did each last in days?
2) How long did each last in weeks?

STREET COMPETITIONS

Skateboarders and aggressive inline skaters get to showcase their talents in "street competitions." The skaters compete on courses that include boxes, quarterpipes, and rails. The obstacles on the courses are made to look and feel like the steps, curbs, hills, and railings that the skaters would use on the street. Each skater usually gets 45 to 60 seconds to move around the course. The skaters must use as many of the different obstacles as possible to perform their tricks. There are no compulsories (moves that the competitors have to do). The competition judges look for creativity, style, level of difficulty of tricks, and the overall flow of the competitor's run.

Go For It!

In skateboarding and skating competitions, five or six judges award points from 0 to 100 to each skater. The lowest and highest marks are thrown out and the remaining marks are averaged. The skater with the highest score wins.

On these pages, you will see some routes that skateboarders and skaters took across a street course. On each route, the skater begins with 100 points (the maximum a skater could earn in a competition). Along the route, you will see all the judges' calculations. Follow each of the routes and do the calculations as you go along. At the end of each route, you will figure out the skater's final score.

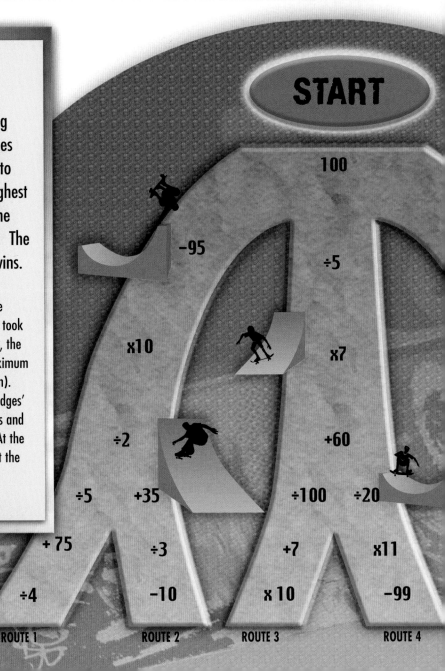

START

100

−95

÷5

x10

x7

÷2

+60

÷5   +35   ÷100   ÷20

+75   ÷3   +7   x11

÷4   −10   x 10   −99

ROUTE 1   ROUTE 2   ROUTE 3   ROUTE 4

Extreme Heroes

In 2002, skateboarder Danny Way set a record for the longest air. He dropped down a 49-foot roll-in into a jump ramp, took off, and flew an incredible 65 feet, landing safely on a landing ramp. The next day, he set a high air record of 18.25 feet off a quarterpipe! Danny once broke his neck in a surfing accident, but he recovered to continue with his amazing skateboarding career.

A skater does a "royale" down a stair handrail.

A skateboarder pulls a "melancholy grab" on a street course.

Math Challenge

A hundred skateboarders were asked how often they bought a new deck (board). Here are the results:

At least once a month	27
Once every three months	30
Once every six months	23
Once every year	20

If the skateboards came from one shop, how many skateboards would be sold in one year to these skateboarders?

An average deck is 7 to 8.5 inches wide, 32 inches long, and 0.4 inches thick.

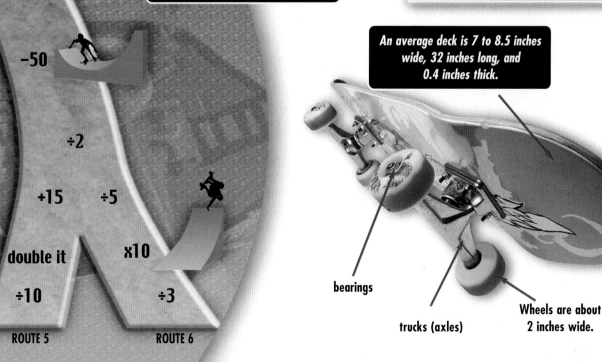

x2

−50

÷2

+15   **÷5**

double it   **x10**

÷10   **÷3**

ROUTE 5   ROUTE 6

bearings

trucks (axles)

Wheels are about 2 inches wide.

THE NEED FOR SPEED

n speed disciplines, inline skaters compete on flat or banked tracks and on roads that are closed down for the race. Skaters of all abilities can take part in "rat races," while top speed skaters compete in championship competitions. During a race, skaters get in a row in pace lines, where they take turns slipstreaming each other to conserve energy. Depending on their tactics, skaters will move from pace line to pace line, slowing down and speeding up again throughout the race. As the end of the race approaches, the skaters will break from their pace lines, make their final moves, and sprint for the finish line.

Go For It!

Speed skaters compete over a variety of distances, from a 300-meter race to a 50-kilometer marathon or even a 161-kilometer endurance race.

A speed skating competition is being held on a track where one lap equals 130 meters. Races are being held over these distances:

a) 500 meters   b) 1,000 meters   c) 1,500 meters   d) 5,000 meters

1) Match these numbers of laps to the races above:

   e) more than 11 but less than 12
   f) more than 3 but less than 4
   g) more than 38 but less than 39
   h) more than 7 but less than 8

2) Which of the four races has a number of laps that is closest to a whole number (a number without fractions)?

3) Some races are being held on a track where one lap equals 400 meters. On this track, how many laps and fractions of a lap must competitors complete in the following races?

   a) 500 meters   b) 1,000 meters   c) 1,500 meters
   d) 3,000 meters   e) 5,000 meters   f) 10,000 meters

Extreme Heroes

In September 2003, skater Jürgen Köhler set a new world inline speed record of 174.8 miles per hour. He achieved this amazing speed by wearing custom-built speed skates worth $8,500 and by holding onto a Suzuki Hayabusa motorcycle! Köhler had to make a number of attempts at reaching his record-breaking speed, and at one point, the Hayabusa actually caught fire! After a hard day's skating, however, a new record was born.

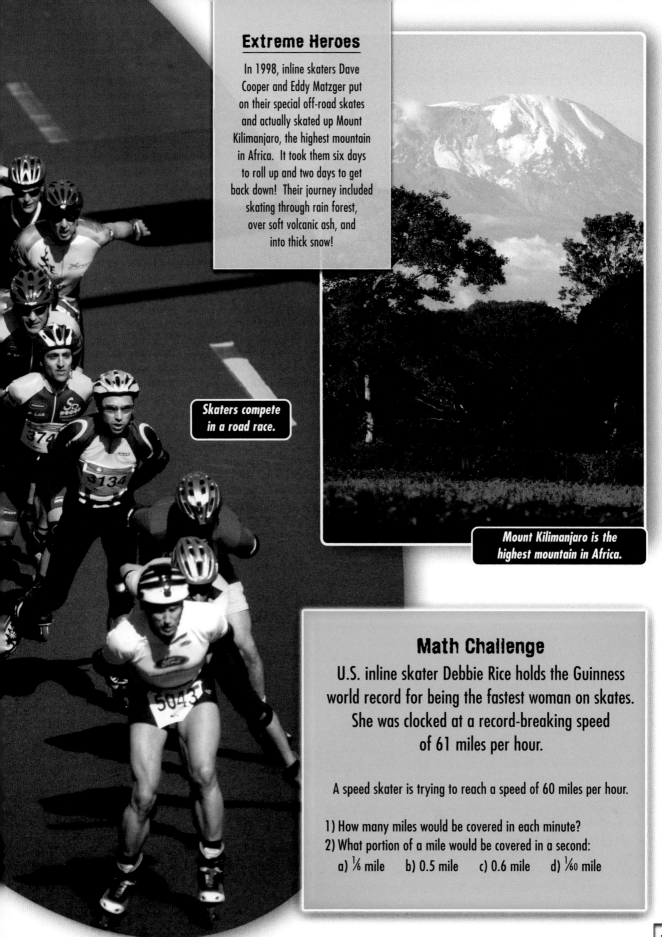

Extreme Heroes

In 1998, inline skaters Dave Cooper and Eddy Matzger put on their special off-road skates and actually skated up Mount Kilimanjaro, the highest mountain in Africa. It took them six days to roll up and two days to get back down! Their journey included skating through rain forest, over soft volcanic ash, and into thick snow!

Skaters compete in a road race.

Mount Kilimanjaro is the highest mountain in Africa.

Math Challenge

U.S. inline skater Debbie Rice holds the Guinness world record for being the fastest woman on skates. She was clocked at a record-breaking speed of 61 miles per hour.

A speed skater is trying to reach a speed of 60 miles per hour.

1) How many miles would be covered in each minute?
2) What portion of a mile would be covered in a second:
   a) ⅙ mile   b) 0.5 mile   c) 0.6 mile   d) ¹⁄₆₀ mile

EXTREME SLOPES

For some snowboarders, only the highest, most dangerous slopes will do. In May 2001, twenty-two-year-old Marco Siffredi became the first person to snowboard down Mount Everest, the highest mountain peak in the world. Marco and his support team climbed to the summit of Everest. Then, at first light, Marco set off alone on his amazing downward journey. It took Marco just two and a half hours to snowboard down Everest. He used nothing more than his snowboard and his own tremendous skill and nerve. Some months later, however, Marco disappeared while trying to repeat his amazing feat. It was a tragic reminder of the danger of extreme sports.

Go For It!

See if you can conquer these questions about extreme slopes and the world's highest mountains.

If Marco Siffredi snowboarded 26,000 feet in 2 hours:

1) How far did he go in 1 hour?

2) What was his speed per hour?

3) In the DATA BOX on page 21, what is the difference in height between the lowest and the highest mountains?

4) Using the DATA BOX on page 21, find the difference in height between the following mountains:

   a) McKinley and Vinson Massif
   b) Everest and Aconcagua
   c) Kilimanjaro and Elbrus

Snowboard Talk

When snowboarders "carve," they are weaving back and forth while going downhill. "Wind lips" are natural jump ramps made from snow blown into place by the wind.

Snowboard Fact

In some of the world's most extreme places, such as Alaska, snowboarders have to be dropped on mountain tops by helicopters because it is so difficult to get to the slopes.

Mega Mountains

Here are the heights (above sea level) of some of the world's highest mountains.
All of these mountains have been conquered by snowboarders!

Mount Everest
(Asia)
29,035 feet

Aconcagua
(South America)
22,834 feet

Mount McKinley
(North America)
20,320 feet

Kilimanjaro
(Africa)
19,340 feet

Elbrus
(Europe)
18,510 feet

Vinson Massif
(Antarctica)
16,864 feet

A snowboarder enjoys some off-piste action.

Math Challenge

Snowboarding trails (routes that can be taken down a mountain) are given different ratings according to their level of difficulty. Snowboarders need to look for these symbols.

EASIEST

MORE DIFFICULT

DIFFICULT

VERY DIFFICULT
(use extreme caution)

The snowboard trail symbols are all symmetrical. A circle has an infinite number of lines of symmetry. How many lines do the other two symbols have?

Snowboard Fact

Snowboarders have been killed by avalanches. When riding off-piste, snowboarders need to check the snow conditions to make sure there is no danger of an avalanche. They often carry small devices called transceivers. If the snowboarders become trapped under an avalanche, the transceiver will give out a signal that can help rescuers find them.

In vert competitions, skaters and skateboarders show what they can do on ramps, halfpipes, and boxes (huge plywood boxes with sloping sides). Skaters are not disqualified if they fall. It's all about going for the most difficult and exciting moves. Vert skating, the story goes, was invented one summer completely by accident. A young skateboarder drained his family's swimming pool so that he and his friends could roll down the side to the deep end on their skateboards. The skaters soon realized that, with enough speed, they could actually ride up the walls of the swimming pool. A whole new range of skating possibilities opened up!

Go For It!

Many skaters and skateboarders actually build their own ramps and boxes so that they can create skate parks in their own backyards!

A group of skaters has been busy building a ramp from plywood. Some leftover pieces of wood have been sorted according to their shapes.

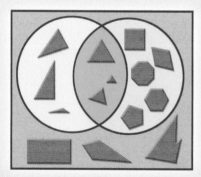

1) Can you tell how these leftover pieces have been sorted?

2) How many triangles can you find here?

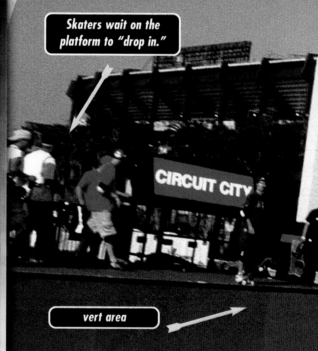

Skaters wait on the platform to "drop in."

vert area

transition

Extreme Heroes

UK skateboarders Joel and Paul Spaven and Jamie Manby have built the world's longest skateboard. The giant board is 23.65 feet long, 11.81 inches wide, and 2.95 inches thick. It cost $895 to build.

COMPETITION HALFPIPE DIMENSIONS
Overall length: 45 feet
Overall width: 16 feet
Vertical height: 11 feet
Flat area between transitions: 16 feet

Obstacle Facts

HALFPIPE This U-shaped ramp has a flat section in the middle and looks like a giant pipe cut in half. The vertical, or "vert," area at the top of each end keeps skaters from drifting away from the ramp when they launch into air tricks.

MINI RAMP A small halfpipe, this ramp is 3 to 6 feet high and has no vert area.

QUARTERPIPE One half of a mini-ramp, this ramp looks like a quarter of a pipe if viewed from the side. It is usually found in the street area at skate parks.

BOWLS These giant, bowl-shaped areas in the ground are usually found at outdoor parks and are made of concrete.

tail grab

Math Challenge

Here are the plans for a ramp. The plans show the length and width of the ramp's surface and the height of the ramp.

1) What is the area of the ramp's surface?
2) What is the perimeter of the ramp's surface?

6 feet

4 feet

2 feet

CIRCUIT CITY.

The lip, or coping, is the metal edge and can be used for grinding.

flat area

O li and Matt say, "Street skating is now illegal in a lot of public places. Many towns and cities around the world have passed laws that ban this type of skating, because it can cause damage to railings, curbs, steps, and park benches. Skate parks offer a safe and legal way for skaters and skateboarders to enjoy their sport without getting into trouble! They are also great places to show off all your best moves and meet up with your friends." Laura says, "Indoor snowboarding facilities allow snowboarders to ride and practice their tricks all year round, even if it's hot and sunny outside."

Go For It!

A new extreme sports center has opened. Some skaters and boarders are checking out the equipment shop and snack bar.

1) Tickets to go into the new center cost $10. With $68, how many tickets could you buy?

2) A meal in the snack bar is $6.99. How many meals can be bought with $40?

3) Tubes of shoegoo are packed in boxes of 70 tubes. If 2/7 of a box is sold, how many are left? If 214 tubes are sold, how many boxes will need to be opened?

4) There are 506 pairs of knee pads in stock, 52 of which are on display. Half of the knee pads not on display are sent to another sports center shop. How many knee pads are sent?

5) Badges are supplied on cards. There are 60 badges on each card. How many rows of badges will there be on each card if the badges are arranged in rows of: a) 10   b) 5   c) 20   d) 3   e) 12

Skate Talk

JAM get a load of skaters together for a skateboarding or aggressive skating session

SESSION the act of skateboarding or inline skating, for example, "session a ramp" or "have a street session"

THRASHED or WRECKED description of equipment worn out from skateboarding or skating.

WALLIE the act of skating onto, up, and over a street object

WALLRIDE the act of skating up a vertical wall

WAX a substance that is used to make obstacles (such as a curb) increasingly slippery for performing various tricks

Snowboard Fact

Snowboarding as we know it today began in 1965, when a Michigan man named Sherman Poppen screwed two skis together. Combining the words "snow" and "surfer," he called his creation a "snurfer."

Gear Guide

IMPACT SHORTS Snowboarders often wear these shorts to provide protection for their hips and lower back. The shorts contain thick padding.

SHOES Skateboarding can cause some serious wear and tear on your shoes. You can buy special skateboarding shoes with ultra-thick rubber soles or use shoegoo on your normal shoes.

SHOEGOO This liquid rubber can be put over holes in your shoes or used to rebuild the soles. The rubber hardens after you spread it on.

SKATE JEANS These wide and baggy jeans give you plenty of room for your knee pads and shin pads, and the bottoms are wide enough to drop over your skates. Skate jeans can also contain extra removable padding.

Math Challenge

A census is taken during the first hour that the new extreme sports center is open. The results are entered on a tally chart.

	Where People Are In The Center
Spectator area	̶H̶H̶ ̶H̶H̶ ̶H̶H̶ ̶H̶H̶ ̶H̶H̶ II
Snowboarding area	̶H̶H̶ ̶H̶H̶ ̶H̶H̶ ̶H̶H̶ ̶H̶H̶ ̶H̶H̶ ̶H̶H̶ III
Street course	̶H̶H̶ ̶H̶H̶ ̶H̶H̶ ̶H̶H̶ ̶H̶H̶ ̶H̶H̶ ̶H̶H̶ ̶H̶H̶ ̶H̶H̶ ̶H̶H̶ I
Vert ramps	̶H̶H̶ ̶H̶H̶ ̶H̶H̶ IIII
Snack bar	̶H̶H̶ ̶H̶H̶ ̶H̶H̶ ̶H̶H̶ ̶H̶H̶ II
Equipment shop	̶H̶H̶ ̶H̶H̶ ̶H̶H̶ ̶H̶H̶
Amusement arcade	̶H̶H̶ ̶H̶H̶ I

1) Which facility is least popular?
2) What is the difference in the number of people who are snowboarding compared with those who are vert skating?
3) How many people are taking part in extreme sports altogether?
4) If 15 more people go for a snack, what will the new snack bar total be?

Laura Berry rides a rail at an indoor snowboarding center.

The world's top extreme athletes get plenty of chances to meet up and compete against each other. Snowboarders compete in the Winter Olympics, and skaters and skateboarders take part in competitions such as the X Games and the Gravity Games. At the X Games, the winning skaters take home cash prizes and medals. Skating and boarding companies usually have teams of ten to twenty boarders or skaters who take part in different competitions and demonstrations around the world. On these pages, you can see snowboarders, skaters, and skateboarders who are showcasing their skills in an event called the Extreme Sports Challenge.

Go For It!

All of the competitors are working hard to impress the crowds and grab the judges' attention!

1) The most steps a skateboarder has cleared so far today is 7. Jez takes off and clears 3 times that many. How many steps has Jez jumped?

2) Ed is trying to land a 900. He falls 9 times but lands the trick 3 times. Show Ed's successes as a fraction of his total number of attempts. Then show the fraction as a decimal.

3) So far on her street run, Charlie has been awarded the following points: 22, 31, 9, 15. How many points must the final judge give her if she is to get a maximum score of 100? Is the amount an odd or even number?

4) Cal has just achieved an amplitude of 323 inches in the "Big Air" competition. How much higher would he need to go, in inches, to reach the highest air record of 30 feet?

5) Judges in sports competitions need to be able to order numbers. Match the following decimal fractions to their corresponding points on the number line:
0.7, 0.2, 1.3, 1.9, 0.6, 1.5, 1.1, 0.8

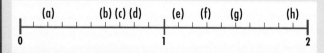

Skateboard Fact

Street luge is strictly for the pros. Riders lay flat on their backs on special, extra-long skateboards. They hurtle down twisting courses at speeds of up to 70 miles per hour. Street lugers wear helmets and full-body leather suits. They also wear rubber-soled shoes, because they use their feet as brakes!

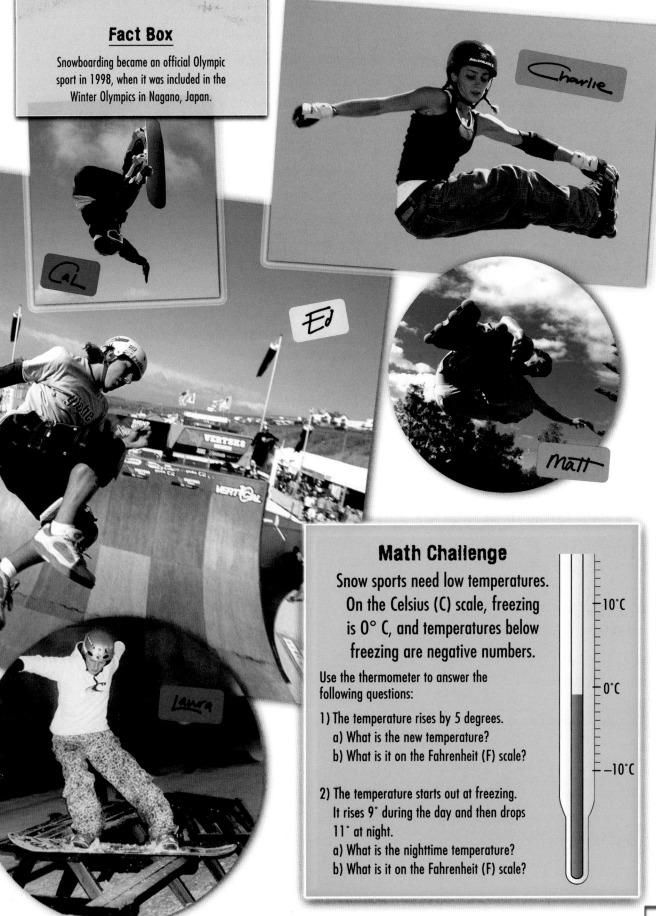

Charlie

Cal

Ed

Matt

Laura

Math Challenge

Snow sports need low temperatures. On the Celsius (C) scale, freezing is 0° C, and temperatures below freezing are negative numbers.

Use the thermometer to answer the following questions:

1) The temperature rises by 5 degrees.
   a) What is the new temperature?
   b) What is it on the Fahrenheit (F) scale?

2) The temperature starts out at freezing. It rises 9° during the day and then drops 11° at night.
   a) What is the nighttime temperature?
   b) What is it on the Fahrenheit (F) scale?

10°C

0°C

−10°C

MATH TIPS

PAGES 6–7

Go For It!

The bars on a bar graph should always be the same width. It is the heights of the bars that are used to compare things. To work with a bar graph, you need to know what each bar stands for. You also need to know the graph's unit of measurement and its scale, such as whether measurements go up by 1s, 2s, 5s, 10s, 100s, 1,000s, or some other amount.

Math Challenge

When rounding numbers, always follow the same rules: round up numbers that end in 5, 6, 7, 8, or 9, and round down numbers that end in 4, 3, 2, or 1. The number 36, for example, would be rounded up to 40, and 32 would be rounded down to 30. When rounding decimal fractions to the nearest whole number, use the same rules. The decimal fraction 3.6, for example, would be rounded to 4, and 3.2 would be rounded to 3.

PAGES 8–9

Angle is a measure of turn and is measured in degrees. The symbol for "degrees" is °.

One complete turn (a complete revolution) is 360°. There are four right angles (90°) in one revolution.

PAGES 10–11

Go For It!

Numbers that put things in order, such as 1st, 2nd, 3rd, and 4th, are ordinal numbers. Counting numbers, such as 1, 2, 3, 4, and so on, are called cardinal numbers.

Math Challenge

TOP TIP: 1 foot equals .3048 meter. Round your results. (See MEASUREMENT CONVERSIONS on page 32)

PAGES 12–13

Go For It!

When adding several small numbers, see if you can begin with the smallest number, look for pairs of numbers that make 10, and find numbers appearing more than once so that you can use multiplication tables. Example: 7 + 7 + 7 is the same as 3 x 7.

Math Challenge

The chart in this section is called a bar line graph. Each bar line represents a rider's amplitude (jump height).

The mean is the average of all the jump heights. Add the jump heights and then divide by the number of heights you added. The median is the middle height in the list of heights. In this case, there is an even number of heights, so add the two middle heights and divide by 2. The mode is the most common height of a jump.

PAGES 14–15

Go For It!

Pictograms

A pictogram is a chart that uses an image to represent a set number of objects or actions. In the pictogram on page 14, an image of a wheel or snowflake represents practicing a trick 10 times. These images can be divided, so a half image represents practicing 5 times.

Math Challenge

There are:
60 minutes in one hour
24 hours in one day
7 days in one week
4–5 weeks in one month
   (Use a calendar to find out the exact
   number of days for a particular month.)

PAGES 20-21

Go For It!

When adding or subtracting large numbers, be sure to line up the numbers so that the hundreds go under the hundreds, the thousands go under the thousands, and so on. Example:

$$2285 + 4193 = 6478$$

$$9785 - 2315 = 7470$$

Math Challenge

Wherever you cut a circle, as long as you go through the center, your cut will be along a line of symmetry.

If a shape can be cut in half so that the halves match, we say that it has a line of symmetry.

PAGES 22-23

Go For It!

This diagram is called a Venn diagram.

In this example, the sets of shapes overlap (intersect).

TOP TIPS: 2D shapes with 3 or more sides are called polygons. A regular 2D shape has all sides the same length.

Math Challenge

TOP TIP: To find the area of a shape, you need to multiply its length and width. The area of the rectangle below, for example, would be 50 square inches.

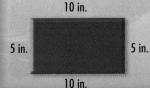

10 in.

5 in.   5 in.

10 in.

To find the perimeter, add all sides. This rectangle, for example, has a perimeter of 30 inches.

PAGES 24-25

Go For It!

When doing calculations of prices, remember that you can round up prices to work out approximate amounts. So $6.99 can be rounded to $7 to make your work easier. Don't forget to take away the cents you added from rounding when you have calculated a final answer.

Math Challenge

A census is a count of people.

A tally is shown as four vertical lines (IIII) and a fifth line drawn diagonally across these lines to make five lines in total. Use your knowledge of the 5 times (multiplication) table to add quickly when using tally marks.

PAGES 26-27

Go For It!

A number line is continuous and extends forever from zero in both directions.

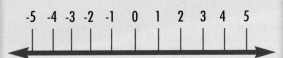

Math Challenge

On the Fahrenheit (F) Scale, freezing is 32°; but temperatures are not negative numbers until they drop below 0°.
0°F = -17.8°C

The formula to convert Celsius temperatures to Fahrenheit is (°C x 1.8) + 32 = °F

The formula to convert Fahrenheit temperatures to Celsius is (°F - 32) ÷ 1.8 = °C

ANSWERS

PAGES 6-7

Go For It!
1) Slightly more than 120 (122)
2) Almost 80 (78)
3) Slightly more than 15 (12 + 5 = 17)
4) The total number of people questioned can be learned from the chart.

Math Challenge
1) Board A offers the biggest range: 55 to 61 inches.
2) Board C is $580 when rounded up to the nearest ten dollars.

PAGES 8-9

Go For It!
1) Powerslide #1 made a ¼ of a turn, which is 90°.
2) Powerslide #2 made a ½ of a turn, which is 180°.
3) The shove-it made a whole turn, which is 360°.

Math Challenge
1) 45°   2) 60°   3) 30°   4) 270°

PAGES 10-11

Go For It!
1) 5 skaters had a time under 26 seconds.
2) Josh, Ant, and Dave had a time over 27 seconds.
3) A skater who finished the sprint in 25.3 seconds would be ranked 5th.
4) • TRACK A would have 21 races.
   • TRACK B would have 10 races.
   • TRACK C would have 17 races.

Math Challenge
1) The height of the jump is approximately 4 meters.
2) a: 3   b: 2   c: 1

PAGES 12-13

Go For It!
1) Alli got the lowest score.
2) Zak did better than Rob in both amplitude and overall impression.
3) Rob got the same score as Zak.
4) Three people: Rob, Zak, and Alli
5) Laura won the competition with 32 points.

Math Challenge
1) The range of amplitudes is 8 feet.
2) mean: 12.6 feet   median: 12.5 feet   mode: 11 feet

PAGES 14-15

Go For It!
1) Trick "a" was practiced:
   Skateboarder: kickflip 40 times
   Inline skater: mute air 60 times
   Snowboarder: rodeo 100 times
2) • Kickflips were practiced 15 more times than 50-50 grinds.
   • Mute airs were practiced 10 more times than Lui Kangs.
   • Rodeos were practiced 35 more times than frontside 540 melons.
3) **Skateboarder:** 135 times
   Inline skater: 175 times
   Snowboarder: 180 times

Math Challenge
1) Inline skate wheels lasted 61 days.
   Snowboards lasted 14 days.
   Skateboard lasted 7 days (168 hours).
2) Inline skate wheels lasted 8 weeks and 5 days.
   Snowboards lasted 2 weeks.
   Skateboard lasted 1 week.

PAGES 16–17

Go For It!

Route 1:	20	Route 2:	10
Route 3:	90	Route 4:	11
Route 5:	18	Route 6:	50

Math Challenge

The shop would sell 510 skateboards.

PAGES 18–19

Go For It!

1) c and e   a and f   d and g   b and h
2) 500 meters
3) **a)** 1¼ laps   **b)** 2 ½ laps   **c)** 3 ¾ laps
   d) 7 ½ laps   **e)** 12 ½ laps   **f)** 25 laps

Math Challenge

1) 1 mile would be covered in each minute.
2) d (1/60 mile in each second)

PAGES 20–21

Go For It!

1) 13,000 feet   2) 13,000 feet per hour
3) 12,171 feet

4)

a) McKinley and Vinson Massif	c) Kilimanjaro and Elbrus
20,320	19,340
-16,864	-18,510
3,456 feet	830 feet

b) Everest and Aconcagua
   29,035
 -22,834
   6,201 feet

Math Challenge

A square has 4 lines of symmetry.   A diamond has 2 lines of symmetry.

PAGES 22–23

Go For It!

1) The leftovers were sorted into the following sets:

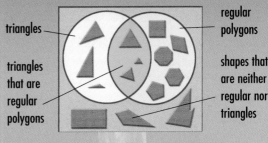

triangles   regular polygons

triangles that are regular polygons   shapes that are neither regular nor triangles

2) You can find 10 triangles:

Math Challenge

1) 24 square feet   2) 20 feet

PAGES 24–25

Go For It!

1) 6 tickets   2) 5 meals
3) 50 tubes, 4 boxes   4) 227 pairs of knee pads
5) a: 6   b: 12   c: 3   d: 20   e: 5

Math Challenge

1) The amusement arcade is the least popular.
2) The difference is 19.
3) 108 people are taking part in sports altogether.
4) The new snack bar total will be 42.

PAGES 26–27

Go For It!

1) 21 steps   2) ¼ = 0.25
3) 23 points (odd)   4) 37 inches

5)   a) 0.2   b) 0.6   c) 0.7   d) 0.8
     e) 1.1   f) 1.3   g) 1.5   h) 1.9

Math Challenge

1) a) 4° C   b) 39.2° F
2) a) -2° C   b) 28.4° F

GLOSSARY

ADRENALINE a chemical produced in your body that increases your heart rate and blood pressure, making you feel a rush of excitement or fear

AERODYNAMIC designed to cut through the air for higher speed and better stability

AGGRESSIVE SKATING a type of inline skating that involves performing tricks such as airs, spins, flips, and grabs on ramps and pipes or over street obstacles

AMPLITUDE the height of a jump, measured as the distance above the lip of a halfpipe

APPROXIMATE close to the exact amount

AVALANCHE a large mass of snow breaking loose and moving down the side of a mountain

BACKSIDE description of a trick in which your back faces the direction you are traveling

BEARINGS devices with a ring of tiny balls that allow wheels to spin freely around axles

CENSUS a count of people

CULTURE the language, art, customs, and beliefs of a certain group of people

DRY SLOPES snowboarding courses with a snowlike substance that can be used in warm temperatures

FRONTSIDE description of a trick in which your front side faces the direction you are traveling

MEAN the average of a set of numbers

MEDIAN a number that is the middle value in a set of numbers

MODE the most common number in a set of numbers

OFF-PISTE snowboarding on a mountain slope that has not been prepared for this activity

PERIMETER the boundary of a shape or area

PROFESSIONAL also called a pro, a person who is paid to do a certain activity, such as take part in extreme sports

SLIPSTREAMING in skating competition, using the reduced air flow directly behind a person to help pull you along

SLOPESTYLE a competition in which snowboarders take three runs down a course filled with rails, jumps, and quarterpipes

STREET SKATING a type of skating that involves using everyday objects such as curbs, park benches, stairs, and handrails to perform tricks

TACTICS in competition, the various strategies used to win

TECHNIQUE the way in which a person performs a particular activity, such as skating

TRUCKS skateboard axles

Trick Talk

Skateboarding

50-50 GRIND Start parallel to an obstacle such as a curb or a rail. Ollie onto the obstacle so both trucks grind against it, then jump off.

BOARDSLIDE This trick is like a grind, but you keep your board 90° to the obstacle, so the middle of your board grinds along the obstacle.

KICKFLIP While you are in the air, kick down on the front of your board and spin it around underneath you.

Snowboarding

BACKSIDE 180 INDY If you are goofy, you spin 180° counterclockwise while your back hand grabs the front of the board between your legs.

RODEO You do a full backflip in the air while spinning 540°.

540 MELON You spin one and a half turns while your front hand grabs the back of the board between your legs.

Measurement Conversions

1 inch = 2.54 centimeters (cm)
1 foot = 0.3048 meter (m)
1 mile = 1.609 kilometers (km)
$°F = (°C \times 1.8) + 32°$